MW01681343

Meet Me At Heaven's Gates

As Inspired by the Holy Spirit
by Ernie Robinson

Meet Me at Heaven's Gates

ISBNN 979-8-9898489-4-2

PAPERBACK

ISBN 979-8-9898489-7-3

DIGITAL

Meet Me At Heaven's Gates

Jesus said to him, "I am the way, the truth, and the life. No one comes to the Father except through Me. (John 14:6 NKJV)

Small Country Church Series
Book 6

DEDICATION

For Uncle Boo Boo

Families age; generational loved ones pass away slowly before our eyes. This has been especially true of my family recently. Loss impacts each of us on a much too regular basis. Since the publication of my last book, "You are Loved in a Small Country Church" our family has suffered the loss of dear friends, old high school classmates, college teammates, two much loved cousins, a dear uncle, a mother, and a father. We are not alone in our loss. As you read this dedication you are doubtlessly thinking of loved ones you have also lost. The loss of parents impacts our lives in an indescribable manner. Yet, it is my dear Uncle Buford to whom I dedicate this book.

When I released my first book, “Words of Forgiveness in a Small Country Church”, I received so much love from my family and friends. Yet, it was the testimony of my uncle which set my heart to tears. You see, he told me this book was the first book he had ever read cover to cover. Not only was he reading my books, but he told me he was sharing them with his friends. As each successive book released, he would call me always providing positive support. Sadly, my last book was sitting on his coffee table waiting unread when he passed from this world to the Arms of a Loving Savior. A Savior who no doubt met him at Heaven's gates with arms open wide.

It is my hope, when my life is complete and my last breath breathed, I will also experience His Wonderous Embrace. I hold in my heart the hope my dear uncle will be among the welcoming committee which meets me at Heaven's Gates with my mother, father, mother-in-law, father-in-law and the many other family and friends who have gone to be with Jesus before me. I have no doubt on that day he will once again provide his positive comments about the books the Lord has blessed me to share.

PREFACE

During my lifetime I have heard humorous stories about Saint Peter waiting for various individuals at heaven's gates. In each account he allowed them to enter heaven after passing a quiz or test. Personally, I find the notion of a grand reunion romantic and very desirable. The thought of generations of loved ones waiting as I ascend the narrow path which leads to Heaven's gates, fills my heart with anticipation.

Yet, the bible does not specifically indicate to us a welcome committee will be waiting for us as we approach on the day of our passing from this world. This concept is of human origin based on the verses in the bible which indicates the huge celebration in heaven when a lost soul turns to Jesus and their place in heaven is affirmed.

> *I tell you that in the same way there will be more rejoicing in heaven over one sinner who repents than over ninety-nine persons who do not need to repent. (Luke 15:7 NIV)*

So where did this idea originate? What if I told you it started with David at the death of his infant son in chapter 12 from the Second Book of Samuel; would you consider it weak testimony? Yet upon learning of the infant's passing, David, King of Israel, shifts from Fasting, Praying and Weeping to an attitude of acceptance and assurance. In this verse it says:

> *But now that he is dead, why should I go on fasting? Can I bring him back again? I will go to him, but he will not return to me. (2 Samuel 12: 23 NIV)*

It is obvious David is very sure he will recognize his son when he reaches Heaven. This agrees with the book of Matthew's account of Jesus' transfiguration, as witnessed by the apostles Peter, James, and John, the brother of James. In this account they instantly recognize both Moses and Elijah who join Jesus to discuss the coming events and his earthly death on the cross. Obviously, Moses (one thousand years earlier) and Elijah (five hundred years earlier) had died before these three apostles were born yet, Peter makes the bold statement of building a shrine to them on the mountain. (Matthew 9:1-7) It also corresponds with the later accounts of Jesus and his apostles during the 40 days following Jesus' resurrection like the account of the road to Emmaus in the book of Luke 24:30-32 (NIV).

"When he was at the table with them, he took bread, gave thanks, broke it and began to give it to them. Then their eyes were opened and they recognized him, and he

disappeared from their sight. They asked each other, "Were not our hearts burning within us while he talked with us on the road and opened the Scriptures to us?"

Can I promise you a welcoming party at Heaven's gates? Well, yes, I believe I can. It might be all of those whom you have loved and who have loved you during your time on this earth. It also might just be one person, Jesus Christ the Son of God. Either way, I guarantee you will find a welcoming committee when you reach the Gates of Pearl at the entrance of Heaven.

God Bless

TABLE OF CONTENTS

DEDICATION
5

PREFACE
9

TABLE OF CONTENTS
15

INTRODUCTION:
17

WHEN NEXT WE MEET
19

MORE THAN JUST BISCUITS
21

HEAVEN IS REAL
47

P.R.A.I.S.E. YE THE LORD
75

LIFE IS LIKE A PSALM
81

PETER GIVES ME HOPE
97

MORE LIKE PETER - (Get Out of the Boat)
125

LET THE SHEPHERDS TESTIFY, GLORIFY, AND PRAISE GOD

141

LOVED AND FORGIVEN
157

ARE YOU IN HIM?
171

INVITATION:
183

ACKNOWLEDGEMENT:
185

APPENDIX
189

LAST WORD
191

ABOUT THE WRITER
193

INTRODUCTION:

On March 22, 2025, at 3:36 pm my precious mother left this world and ran into the arms of Her Lord Jesus Christ. Despite having been bedridden during her last 4 years upon this earth, she ran to him on legs as strong as a world class sprinter. Of this fact I have no doubt.

I have no doubt about one other fact. She is now waiting for the day when my time upon this earth is completed, and I go to join her. To do so, I must unlock the secret to opening Heaven's Gates. Join me as I pursue this wondrous secret. The secret of Eternal Life in Heaven with Jesus the Christ, the Son of God!

WHEN NEXT WE MEET

(A poem dedicated to our loved ones)

When next we meet at Heaven's Gate,
O how we will grin and smile.
Laughter and Joy will be our song,
as together we rush to each other's arms.

When next we meet, walking hand in hand,
to God's Throne room we shall go.
To hear those precious words, spoken so
long ago,
enter in my precious child, enter in.

by Ernie Robinson

MORE THAN JUST BISCUITS

As if an alarm clock had gone off, she rose from her night of restless sleep. It was time to get up. She had gotten out of bed at this same time since she was a girl. Raised a farmer's daughter, the oldest in her family, she had been expected to serve all of her life it seemed. From those early years when she cared for the younger siblings to the years standing at her mother's side learning and helping to prepare family meals. Now she cared for her own family. It was time to start the day.

The living room and kitchen of her house adjoined one another, so she turned on the television to her favorite religious channel. She kept the volume low enough not to disturb her family but high enough so she could hear the words of the pastor. As the television came to life, she heard the pastor ask his audience a question:

> "Who is this who can take people who passed through the dark night of sorrow and suffering and transform them into surgeons, teachers, musicians, scientists, preachers, scholars, and statesmen? Who is this who can take the sons and daughters of poverty and limited means and bring them into lives of promise, prosperity, and

> potential? Who is this who can look upon injustice all over the world and infuse the people living under oppression and injustice with the belief that things can be better, then equip those people to go about doing the work that will make their world a better place? Who is this? Only a sovereign God can do something like that."

It was Palm Sunday; unlike Easter, there would not be a huge crowd of visitors and "once a year" Christians at church this morning. But most of the regulars will make a point to be there. Just like Easter morning, the preacher will have a special message.

She needed to get Sunday's breakfast started. From the living room she heard the TV preacher ask those in attendance another question:

"Who is this?"

She thought to herself, what a wonderful question. She pondered, I wonder if that was the same question the crowd held on that day when Jesus rode that donkey into Jerusalem to start holy week? She reasoned to herself being no one else was yet awake, this is a question waiting for each one of us to answer.

There were no measuring cups on the counter, just a large bowl, a bag of flour, cows milk fresh from the cow earlier that morning, a glass of cool water and of course lard. She counted in her head the number of biscuits needed for breakfast then began to dip flour from the bag. Five no, six hands full of flour went into the bowl then she stopped and stared at the tub of lard. She thought back to the days when she would help her great grandmother make biscuits for the family. The recipe passed down from mother to daughter for more generations than she could remember. She brushed her hands off on the towel which lay on the kitchen counter and then plunged her hand into the tub. As if through muscle memory she collected the correct amount of lard and the process of marrying it to the flour began. Slowly but surely, she worked the lard into the flour until the consistency met her expectations. Splash went the milk as it in turn entered the bowl, maybe a tad bit of water too she thought. She worked the mixture together until the dough formed just the way her mother had shown her so many times before. She heard the preacher say from the other room:

> The story boils down to an encounter between two groups of people. Some in the crowd knew who Jesus was, they had heard all the stories about Him. When Jesus

rode into Jerusalem on the first Palm Sunday, this first group responded by crying out, "Blessed is He who comes in the name of the Lord" and "Hosanna." However, there were others in Jerusalem that day who had no idea who Jesus was; they were probably the overwhelming majority of the residents and religious pilgrims in the city. Their response was not to line His path with palm branches and a garment-laden welcome mat; their response was dismissive and full of contempt: Who is this?

On one hand, says Matthew, there were people who were laying their garments on the ground and tearing off branches from trees to create a kind of "red-carpet arrival" for the Man they believed to be the Messiah, the Son of God, the Son of David. They stood and cheered hoping Jesus would be an earthly king who would overthrow the Romans and re-establish Israel to its former glory as it enjoyed in the days of David and Solomon. These were the people who were making all the noise and creating all the uproar; they were welcoming the change they thought Jesus' arrival was about to create.

On the other hand, there were the urban and sophisticated citizens of the bustling city of Jerusalem who had no idea what was going on that day. It may be hard for us to believe today as we live in a world of global communication bringing the most remote locations on earth right into our own living rooms. Sadly, many of the people in Jerusalem had never heard about Jesus before that day. There were, after all, twelve gates into and out of the city

> of Jerusalem. Depending on the gate through which you entered, it was possible for most people in the city to have no idea that anything was going on across town. Most who observed the events of Palm Sunday had no idea who this was at the center of all the commotion.

The process is called "kneading the dough." As she worked the dough, she thought back to Sunday morning bible school lessons from long ago. She remembered how the children of Israel had to rush to make bread the night of the exodus. That night they made bread for the Passover meal without yeast and added bitter herbs for taste. She thought to herself, maybe I should add just a pinch of salt, as her attention returned to the biscuits. Not to loose yet, not to stiff, she then began the process of pinching off handfuls of dough and rolling them into a ball. She had sprinkled flour on the parchment paper lying on the counter and one by one the balls of flour would be rolled and kneaded into the perfect shape. Unlike the bread of the Passover, her biscuits had the perfect amount of yeast already added by the company where she had purchased her flour. She took the parchment paper and laid it across a baking sheet careful not to dump any loose flour in the floor. She gave the sheet a little shake to evenly distribute the flour and then placed the biscuits upon the paper. She carefully spaced the balls one inch apart forming a perfect square in the center of the sheet. She had preheated the oven to 400 degrees as she placed the biscuits on a center rack. As she lifted her head, she heard the preacher's message continue from the other room:

> Who is this may have been posed by some who were unfamiliar with Jesus. On the one hand, it might have been a tone of contempt and derision. It was as if they were looking down on Jesus as a country boy who was not ready for the big city. As he entered the city that morning, he was not dressed in

> clothes from the latest fashion. He did not move with the pompous swagger or confidence of the leaders they frequently saw moving through their city.

She had ten or so minutes to scramble the eggs and mix up some gravy. The bacon and sausage had already finished cooking and were resting on plate covered in paper towels to absorb any excess grease. Her thoughts turned away from the preacher on TV to the story of Martha and Mary on the occasion when Jesus came to visit his friend Lazarus. Like Martha, she was in the kitchen alone working on the hardy breakfast meal for her family. She smiled and thought about those who soon would rush in to fix their plates about her stove. The voice of the preacher returned to her ears as she heard him say:

> He was dressed in common robes. Worse yet, instead of riding on a white stallion as a Roman conqueror would do, Jesus came into Jerusalem riding on a donkey. The people would've been aware of the prophecy found in Zechariah 9:9, the one which foretold of the Messiah who would ride into Jerusalem in that way, but they were unable or unwilling to connect the Messianic prophecy to the Man

> they saw before them. Hear the scorn in their voices: Who is this? Hear the sneer and contempt in their voices as they disdainfully dismiss Jesus: Who is this?

Upon the family's arrival they would find their traditional Sunday morning breakfast. A patty of sausage, two slices of bacon, two biscuits with a scoop of gravy on top and finally a helping of fluffy, scrambled eggs. There would also be store bought orange juice, milk, and of course coffee was waiting, as she alerted her loved ones to the time, "let's get washed up". As she returned to the kitchen, she heard the preacher ask his congregation:

Who is this who can cause people to take off their coats and lay them on the ground so His donkey could walk over them? Who is this for whom people would tear palm branches off the trees to create a carpet? None of the priests of the Temple were welcomed in this way. Certainly, no Roman, not even the governor, Pontius Pilate had received such a hero's welcome. Imagine, therefore, some people in the city were impressed by what they saw, and they wanted to know more about the Man who had caused such a response.

The timer went off alerting her to the biscuit's completion. She did not really need a timer as the smell of fresh bread filled the kitchen. She stood to the side and opened the oven door; a dozen beautifully browned biscuits were set on the cookie sheet ready to be served. Using her dish towel, she pulled the cookie sheet covered by the lightly browned parchment paper from the oven. A large wooden bowl stood waiting to receive the biscuits. In they went one by one until all were in the bowl then, by habit having seen her mother and grandmother before her do so, she placed the dish towel overtop the bowl. The dish towel not only kept the biscuits warm it held the moisture into the freshly baked bread keeping it soft and flaky. From the adjoining room the TV preacher continued:

> The question of Palm Sunday remains the question for us to consider on this Sunday 2,000 years later: Who is this? This was not simply a matter of interest for the residents of Jerusalem; this is the question that is still being asked and answered today. Who is Jesus, and why should we pay attention to His teachings? Who is Jesus, and why have so many people put their lives under His authority? Who is this who can achieve such marvelous

> things? The world is full of books having a shelf life of but a few months or years, after which nobody reads them again. Yet Jesus remains as relevant today as when He walked the earth. Jesus…

A quick check and a few quick stirs to turn the eggs, a few quick stirs of the gravy as it simmered. Back and forth she went until the gravy was a perfect light brown and the eggs were just done enough to be fluffy but not scorched top or bottom. Off the heat and straight into granny's heavy glass bowls for both, then came the call her sons and husband had been waiting for… As she walked into the living room to turn the television off, she heard the final question of the preacher in his morning service:

> Who is this who could take men such as Peter, James and John and turn those fishermen from Capernaum into household names in every corner of the earth? Who is this that could take a Pharisee named Saul—an opponent to Christianity—and in a single encounter on the Damascus Road turn him into the chief proponent of the gospel of Jesus Christ, the very Man whose name he once had attempted to abolish? Who is this who can take people who passed

through the dark night of sorrow and suffering and transform them into surgeons, teachers, musicians, scientists, preachers, scholars and statesmen? Who is this who can take the sons and daughters of poverty and limited means and bring them into lives of promise, prosperity, and potential? Who is this who can look upon injustice all over the world and infuse the people living under oppression and injustice with the belief that things can be better, then equip those people to go about doing the work that will make their world a better place? Who is this? This is something only a sovereign God can do!

As the family came down the steps from their bedrooms, they saw their mother standing in front of the TV. Each one in turn joined her as they listened to the preacher finish his Palm Sunday sermon. They hadn't heard the questions asked over the past 20 minutes or so. All they knew was their mother was standing silently in front of the television. They stood at her side as he finished.

Jesus, the Man they loved on Palm Sunday, condemned, killed and buried on Good Friday, but who left his grave on Easter morning with all power in His hands. Jesus, The Lord of heaven and earth. Jesus, the Lord of the past, present and future. Jesus, the Lord of the living, and the dead, Lord of the greatest and least. Jesus: LORD OF ALL! The next time somebody asks "Who is this", whether he or she speaks with contempt or amazement—this is what you can tell them, "He is the Lord. He is risen from the dead, and lives forever more. One day soon, at His name, every knee shall bow and every tongue confess, Jesus Christ is Lord! That is who Jesus is".

Her family sat quietly at the table waiting for her to finish her plate and join them. She looked at her eldest son as they all took hands, why don't you say grace this morning. "Yes mother" was his reply. Normally, mom or dad came out of his mouth when addressing his parents, but prayer time was just different. It was a time for reverence, both to parents, as well as to God.

God, we thank you that you love and provide for our daily needs. We thank you for watching over each of us as we go through our day, keeping us safe from harm and blessing us with Your Love. Father, we thank you for this food which we are about to eat.

Bless it so it will nourish our bodies.
Thank you for blessing each member
of our family. In Jesus Name, Amen.

She looked about the table at her husband and sons as they began to eat and thought to herself how blessed she was to have this wonderful family of men in her life. She whispered a soft prayer of her own, thanksgiving to her Loving Father for the blessings He had placed on her life because of a man named Jesus.

HEAVEN IS REAL

Loss is very difficult. It overwhelms during the quiet hours when we are alone. It is ever present waiting for our attention to slip from what is at hand to what if. We are all dealing with loss whether we want to admit it or not. As I mentioned before, my dear mother recently passed from this world. I have no doubt about her destiny. If my father had been the captain, it was my mother who was truly the anchor of our family. She held fast to Jesus and insisted we attend church each time the doors opened. During my youth there were things I could count on regardless of our family's financial pressures. There would be breakfast on the table every day of the week and there would be four family members seated at the table each morning. Sunday's and Wednesdays we would be seated in the pews of a small country church learning about Jesus and his everlasting love.

Dementia had slowly robbed my sweet mother of her faculties; it is the nature of Dementia and Alzheimer's. Thankfully, her sweet disposition and kindness were unaffected. As she lay in her bed, rolling from side to side unable to find a comfortable position, I sat quietly. She rolled in my direction and our eyes fixed upon one another and she asked me, "Would you read me one of the chapters from your book? The one about forgiveness.""Do you have a favorite chapter", I replied. "I love the one about lost and found, can you read that one to me?"

She kept copies of each of the books I had written in the small cabinet next to her bed. I opened the drawer and took that first book, "Words of Forgiveness in a Small Country Church" out of the drawer, then closed the drawer softly. I opened the pages of the book to chapter three and began to read.

> *"Psalm 144:13 (NIV) Our barns will be filled with every kind of provision.*

Our sheep will increase by thousands,

by tens of thousands in our fields;

JESUS WELCOMES SINNERS:

Now the tax collectors and sinners were all gathering around to hear Jesus. But the Pharisees and the teachers of the law muttered, “This man welcomes sinners and eats with them.” Then Jesus told them this parable: “Suppose one of you has a hundred sheep and loses one of them. Doesn’t he leave the ninety-nine in the open country and go after the lost sheep until he finds it? And when he finds it, he joyfully puts it on his shoulders and goes home. Then he

> calls his friends and neighbors together and says, 'Rejoice with me; I have found my lost sheep.' I tell you that in the same way there will be more rejoicing in heaven over one sinner who repents than over ninety-nine righteous persons who do not need to repent."

During the time I was reading, her gaze remained fixed and she lay completely motionless hanging on every word. I had grown up chasing a ball unlike my two brothers who were accomplished students who held spots at or near the top of their respective graduating class. They each had spent their lives on honor roles and Dean's lists. Me, not so much. In fact, the first time my name appeared on the dean's list from college, the article had been trimmed with care, framed, and proudly placed on top of the entertainment center in the family room. During my youth I never read aloud to anyone for any reason, not even during my years at Morehead State University. Not until God called me to stand in the gap at Ringos Mills Christian Church did I begin to read aloud to an audience. Now here I was 15 years later, sitting at her bedside reading a full chapter from the book "He" had blessed me to write. As I finished the story from chapter three, I looked up to see a tear roll slowly down her cheek. Then, as if someone had flipped a switch, she returned to shifting positions, rolling from side to side. As tears started to form, I looked away and noticed one of her beloved caregivers standing in the doorway. She too had tears in her eyes. The origin of her tears was from the news she was about to share. Deep inside me I hoped the story from the book had touched her heart. Sadly, I knew better.

“Ernie, could you step out in the hallway for a second"? The words which came next are words every child dread, “Your mother is dying, and she is in tremendous pain. We (the staff of caregivers who loved and cared for mom during the family’s absence) believe you should consider calling in hospice." Hospice, the wonderful group of caregivers who provide measured medical comfort to loved ones who are standing at death's door, sitting quietly to assist both with the passing and the loss felt by the family. Hospice, the word stabs like a dull knife passing through the flesh. Instantly my mind conjured a memory of their warmth and help when my wife had lost her mother. Hospice, the word cuts through the denial and painted for me a picture of release. Something I was not ready to endure. Yet, standing in the hallway listening to the bed creak and moan as she rolled slowly from side to side searching for release from the pain, I knew my time on earth with her was ending. My thoughts flashed back to simpler days.

I had a blessed youth. Loving and supportive parents, a younger brother who was a friend and a confident. But as with all things of this world time passes and we must move forward. The years passed too quickly and soon it would be my time to go out into this world. I would start my own family, and together we would make our way as best as possible. I often longed for the simplicity of those early days under the care of my loving mother and father. I think most people long for what we perceive as simpler times. With my mother's impending passing I caught myself thinking, what will Heaven be like? I hope you the reader, will not consider this a selfish thought but rather one commonly shared when related to the passing of a beloved family member. Whatever the reason, this was my state of mind. As the title of the book suggests, it is my sincere hope to see them awaiting me, especially my dear mother at Heaven's Gates, when my time concludes upon this earth

Heavens versus Heaven:

The Bible refers to the sky that covers the earth as the heavens, small "h." This is the realm of birds and clouds that surround the entire earth. Humanity has studied the heavens in great detail defining its many layers, functions, and properties. We have fixed our thoughts on the clouds, their many shapes and sizes. We study their composition and marvel at the destructive power they can hold. We write poems and post pictures of their shapes. Yet the clouds make up but a tiny portion of the heavens. Take a ride on a modern jet passenger plane and you will quickly find yourself traveling at such heights that you can look down on the top of the clouds. I could write about the different layers of our atmosphere but quickly your eyes would begin to glaze. The truth is humankind has decided we fully understand why it exists and what we must do to maintain its delicate balance in the role of preserving our lives. Yet I wonder if we truly understand anything more than the basics. This is the first heaven.

The second heaven is where the stars, the sun, and the moon reside. This is the space beyond the earth, and it covers the entire universe. For most of my life I have been blessed to live in eastern Kentucky where bright streetlights and large buildings do not obstruct the grandeur of God's magnificent creation. My memory takes me back to those unbearably hot summer nights of August, when we lived in a simple trailer behind the Garrison Elementary school. My sweet mother would take one of her heavy quilts outside and spread it upon the ground and tell stories of her youth, as my brother and I counted the many stars and constellations in this heaven. Humanity has been looking up and telling stories about these bright lights in the sky since the dawn of our creation. This layer of heavens extends far beyond what the human eye can see. It is only with the help of powerful telescopes such as Hubble and James Webb Space Telescopes we can truly appreciate the enormity of God's full creation.

But the bible tells us of a third heaven, one unseen by human eyes. A place, with very few exceptions, where only those who have passed from this world have seen. It is the residence of God, including Jesus Christ who sits at His right hand. A place where gates of pearl await those blessed to follow His path to eternal life.

> *It is doubtless not profitable for me to boast. I will come to visions and revelations of the Lord: I know a man in Christ who fourteen years ago—whether in the body I do not know, or whether out of the body I do not know, God knows—such a one was caught up to the third heaven. And I know such a man—whether in the body or out of the body I do not know, God knows— how he was caught up into Paradise and heard inexpressible*

words, which it is not lawful for a man to utter. (2 Corinthians 12:1-4 NKJV)

I said there were few who witnessed heaven while still living upon the earth. Few is not zero thus, let me share with you a list of those mentioned as "Biblical Eyewitnesses to Heaven".

- *Elijah was caught up into heaven, taken up in a whirlwind; he never tasted death (II Kings 2:1-12).*
- *Enoch who was said to have walked with God, was taken up into heaven without ever tasting death. (Genesis 5:24)*

- *The apostle John saw heaven through an open door so that he might see and record in the book of Revelation some of the things he saw in heaven (Revelation. 4:1).*
- *Paul was on the Damascus Road on his way to persecute Christians, He saw heaven open up. (Acts 9:3-4)*
- *and of course, Jesus*

You may have read or heard of someone who experienced a near death situation and witnessed a glimpse of heaven for themselves. Personally, I have met only one person with such an experience. This person had never accepted Jesus as his savior at the time of his experience. Shortly thereafter he was baptized and has been a faithful member of church ever since. To hear him recount his experience will make your hair stand on end in fright. Yet others describe such a realm beyond earthly description. Several describe meetings with loved ones in heaven, their family, friends, and even their pets. This is difficult to prove, yet the sheer number of those who have seen heaven (or hell) and came back from death is hard to refute; only they themselves know this for certain (and God of course). But the Bible does describe what heaven is like in the scriptures. It is, from the human standpoint, indescribable. 1 Corinthians 2:9 (NIV) says:

> *However, as it is written: "What no eye has seen, what no ear has heard, and what no human mind has conceived"— the things God has prepared for those who love him—*

How does the bible describe Heaven?

- *There is a constant chant of holy angels that are continually proclaiming Holy, Holy, Holy over the throne of God. The Mercy Seat in heaven where God sits is surrounded by magnificent angels full of glory and power that proclaim and bless the holy name of God without ceasing.*

- *There are beasts, full of eyes, with six wings and neither rest day or night in their proclaiming the holiness of God (Rev. 4:8-11).*

John, who was "carried away" to heaven in chapter 4 of the book of Revelation gives the best description of heaven I know of; at least the heaven seen by those who are Christ's today. The Apostle John describes Heaven based on his vision during his time on the Island of Patmos. John does not specifically say why he had been sent to the penal colony at Patmos. However, he was widely accepted as the primary Christian leader at the time and would have spoken against the worship of Emperor Domitian as a god. (However) Nearly 100 years after John's death in Ephesus, the Christian writer Tertullian wrote John had been exiled to Patmos because the emperor (Domitian) had set a large vat of boiling oil in the center of the Coliseum and intended to make John's execution very public, and very painful. It was his intent to lower him slowly into the oil alive. Tertullian continued the story by saying, the problem was John did not die, rather he continued to preach the Gospel of Jesus Christ to all who were in attendance. He continued to do so until he was removed from the coliseum by the Roman guards. It was this embarrassment that led the emperor to exile him. Whether this is true or not we will not know until we reach Heaven and ask him ourselves. Regardless, John says he was sent there because of his testimony concerning Jesus as the Christ, the Son of the one and only God. Let me share John's words from the Isle of Patmos about Heaven:

> *And he carried me away in the Spirit to a mountain great and high, and showed me the Holy City, Jerusalem, coming down out of heaven from God. It shone with the glory of God, and its brilliance was like that of a very precious jewel, like a jasper, clear as crystal. It had a great, high wall with twelve gates, and with*

twelve angels at the gates. On the gates were written the names of the twelve tribes of Israel. There were three gates on the east, three on the north, three on the south and three on the west. The wall of the city had twelve foundations, and on them were the names of the twelve apostles of the Lamb.

The angel who talked with me had a measuring rod of gold to measure the city, its gates and its walls. The city was laid out like a square, as long as it was wide. He measured the city with the rod and found it to be 12,000 stadia '1,400 miles' in length, and as wide and high as it is long.

The angel measured the wall using human measurement, and it was 144 cubits [that is 200 feet!] thick. The wall was made of jasper, and the city of pure gold, as pure as glass. The foundations of the city walls were decorated with every kind of precious stone. The first foundation was jasper, the second sapphire, the third agate, the fourth emerald, the fifth onyx, the sixth ruby, the seventh chrysolite, the eighth beryl, the ninth topaz, the tenth turquoise, the eleventh jacinth, and the twelfth amethyst. The twelve gates were twelve pearls, each gate made of a single pearl. The great street of the city was of gold, as pure as transparent glass.

I did not see a temple in the city, because the Lord God Almighty and the Lamb are its temple. The city does not need the sun or the moon to shine on it, for the glory of God gives it light, and the Lamb is its lamp. The nations will walk by its light, and the kings of the earth will bring their splendor into it. On no day will its gates ever be shut, for there will be no night there. The glory and honor of the nations will be brought into it. Nothing impure will ever enter it, nor will anyone who does what is shameful or deceitful, but only those

> *whose names are written in the Lamb's book of life.* Revelation 21:10-27 (NIV)

So, the question becomes, can you see Heaven? Acts 2:38 - 39 (NKJV) provides us with instructions directly from Jesus through the Apostle Peter. Here it says:

> *Then Peter said to them, "Repent, and let every one of you be baptized in the name of Jesus Christ for the remission of sins; and you shall receive the gift of the Holy Spirit. For the promise is to you and to your children, and to all who are afar off, as many as the Lord our God will call."*

You see; there is no other way to get to heaven but by the Son of God. Getting to heaven is a one-way trip for most of us. Like the story of the rich man and Lazarus, the rich man who died without Christ is forever denied access to heaven and to God. It is an everlasting location from which no one can ever leave. It is a place my friend described as he spoke through tears of fear which his heart still felt years after his experience. His description closely aligned with the passage from the book of Revelation 21:7-8 (NIV) showing the fate of those not going to heaven:

> *"Those who are victorious will inherit all this, and I will be their God and they will be my children. But the cowardly, the unbelieving, the vile, the murderers, the sexually immoral, those who practice magic arts, the idolaters and all liars—they will be consigned to the fiery lake of burning sulfur. This is the second death."*

Now, it is my most sincere hope and prayer that no one would ever go there, and I am so thankful I know my precious mother's eternal destination. For us, there is one surefire way to go to heaven. By accepting

Jesus as your Lord and Savior. Just as my mother had done as a young girl, as my cousin Suzie and I did that summer of my 10th birthday in a small country church. Why, because Jesus (who was God's precious only Son) died after living a perfect life. He spilled His blood to take the Holy Father's wrath upon Himself. This is the gift that Jesus gave to me and you from the cross. It is my sincere hope if you have not made your decision for Christ, you will do so today, before it is too late. Think of it like this, who is standing at Heaven's gate today hoping you will join them someday when your time on earth is over. Doesn't their hope matter to you?

P.R.A.I.S.E. YE THE LORD

It is so hard to praise the Lord when someone you love is suffering. To say otherwise would be a disservice to everyone who has ever sat at a loved one's bedside as they lay dying. For my precious mother, Hospice started out wonderfully. We had called my youngest brother Will, a doctor in the Atlanta area, and together the three of us agreed to start the hospice process. Will planned to visit the day after the Hospice treatments were to begin. Mom's face lit up as he and his three children walked into the room. With the help of the pain reducing medicines, she was completely lucid and fully returned to her loving self. She talked to the kids about their lives and told stories about holding each of them when they were first born and how she had traveled to their home during the first week of each of their lives so their mother could rest and recover from childbirth. They spent a wonderful day together. The next couple of days made us question our decision as she fully returned to the mother we had known in our youths. She talked and laughed, told stories of growing up as the oldest daughter of a sharecropper on farms around Richmond, Kentucky. She recounted for the family about the winter after the boys came home from World War II and how the farm they had been working was taken from her dad and given to a returning veteran. She didn't speak out of bitterness but thankfulness as her grandmother and mother had cleaned out the family chicken coop and turned it into a makeshift bedroom where the family would sleep at night under a pile of quilts. Although my grandfather (her dad) was embarrassed and felt it was the worst job in town, he had secured a job picking up trash. He did what it took to put food on his family's table and get them out of the chicken coop as quickly as possible. A man with a third-grade education worked hard every day of his life to provide for his family. He lived his American dream with his beautiful family of three daughters and a son. He passed at the age of eighty being loved and respected. Not because of his great riches but, because of his reputation of being a good, honest, God-fearing man who raised a good family. Mom was so proud of her daddy, you could hear it in her voice and the stories she told before she left us.

It was those hours of lucidity for which I was most thankful as the time drew near to say goodbye. It is so easy to Praise when life is good, yet this is when we are most likely to be too preoccupied to remember His goodness. As the days of the week wore by, the effects of dementia returned. Her loving nature was swallowed by a darkness we did not understand. During her final hours as she struggled for each breath, we each in turn held her hand. Kissing her forehead we each whispered, “I Love You Mom.” I cannot speak to the words whispered in her ear by the others, but my final words to her, beside the statement of my eternal love for her, was to make a request. I simply asked her to wait for me by the gates, so her face is the first one I see when I arrive. I give praise to my Father in Heaven for sending His One and Only Son, through my faith in Him, I have the hope of a wonderful reunion someday when my time on earth is complete.

LIFE IS LIKE A PSALM

Psalm 147 (NIV)

Praise the Lord.

How good it is to sing praises to our God, how pleasant and fitting to praise him! The Lord builds up Jerusalem; he gathers the exiles of Israel. He heals the brokenhearted and binds up their wounds. He determines the number of the stars and calls them each by name. Great is our Lord and mighty in power; his understanding has no limit. The Lord sustains the humble but casts the wicked to the ground.

Sing to the Lord with grateful praise; make music to our God on the harp. He covers the sky with clouds; he supplies the earth with rain and makes grass grow on the hills. He provides food for the cattle and for the young ravens when they call. His pleasure is not in the strength of the horse, nor his delight in the legs of the warrior; the Lord delights in those who fear him, who put their hope in his unfailing love.

Extol the Lord, Jerusalem; praise your God, Zion.

He strengthens the bars of your gates and blesses your people within you. He grants peace to your borders and satisfies you with the finest of wheat. He sends his command to the earth; his word runs swiftly. He spreads the snow like wool and scatters the frost like ashes. He hurls down his hail like pebbles. Who can withstand his icy blast? He sends his word and melts them; he stirs up his breezes, and the waters flow. He has revealed his word to Jacob, his laws and decrees to Israel. He has done this for no other nation; they do not know his laws.

Praise the Lord.

As I reflect back on my time with my mother and father, I remember I have never met anyone who did not appreciate praise. Even simple tasks such as mowing the lawn or washing the car deserve praise. Men, how often have you thanked your wife for preparing your meal or washing your dishes? I am quick with a compliment about the quality of Angie's cooking, yet I often forget to thank her for the spotless kitchen she keeps or the clean dishes I eat from. Just as I carefully mow straight lines in my yard hoping it visually meets my neighbor's approval, I should remember to provide complements to those whose efforts make my life easier. Why would our Father in Heaven who pours out blessings upon us daily be any different? Join me as I reflect on the concept and importance of the word Praise.

P = Presence

"Let us come into his presence with thanksgiving; let us make a joyful noise to him with songs of praise! For the Lord is a great God, and a great King above all gods." Psalms. 95:2-3

R = Renewal

"In His presence, there is fullness of joy." Psalms. 16:11

A = All Knowing

The LORD looks from heaven; He sees all the sons of men; From His dwelling place He looks out on all the inhabitants of the earth, He who fashions the hearts of them all, He who understands all their works. (Psalm 33:13-15)

I = Inside

“He inhabits the praises of His people.” Psalms. 22:3

S = Salvation

“About midnight Paul and Silas were praying and singing hymns to God, and the prisoners were listening to them, and suddenly there was a great earthquake, so that the foundations of the prison were shaken. And immediately all the doors were opened, and everyone's bonds were unfastened.” Acts 16:25-26

E = Everyone

Acts 2:21 And everyone who calls on the name of the Lord will be saved.
(Unconditional Forgiveness)

I really love when smart people take the letters of a word to create an acrostic. In this case it is a wonderful way to offer praise to our Father in Heaven. Speaking of praising our Father, I remember a story told to me by my mother. The story is from the Old Testament. It seems a King of Israel found himself in a tight spot and did not know what to do. He tried to solve the problem through diplomacy, which did not work. He tried everything he could think of, but the problem kept growing. Finally, but one solution remained. The solution he should have tried first; he turned the problem over to God. Let us look at the solution together.

2 Chronicles 20: verses 6 &12 (NIV)

O Lord, the God of our fathers . . . Power and might are in Your hand. . .. We are powerless before this great multitude . . . nor do we know what to do, but our eyes are on You.

At this point in history the nation of Judah had just received horrible news. A vast army was gathering to destroy them, and King Jehoshaphat had no idea how they could survive such a vicious attack. Finally, he turned to God and God quickly answered his prayer. God's answer probably puzzled the king. God sent a message to the king, "the battle was not Judah's but His." Then the Lord set up the battle plan. Instead of warriors leading the way, God instructed the king to place the choir up front and march into battle singing praises to His name. (God's, not the King's) I would have loved to have seen the king's face when he heard that plan. No arrows, no tar-and-pitch rockets were to take flight, only praises to God.

Regardless of what he felt inside, the king's actions demonstrated he trusted God as he obeyed the Lord. Before the army of Judah reached the battlefield, God had thrown the enemy in to such confusion that they turned on one another. The army of Judah never lifted a bow because God defeated its enemies. Mom would always point to the power of faith after finishing this story. Faith was very important to her and she wanted us to share in her trust and faith in our Lord.

Have I mentioned I grew up loving to chase a ball? When you are young, competition feels just like life or death. Or at least this was the way it seemed in my family. My dad, Coach Bill Robinson, possessed a gift, a skill of taking young men and getting them to perform above what they recognized as their own ability. Year after year he managed to eke out victories with undersized and under skilled young men on the gridiron surfaces of Eastern Kentucky. His ability to coax wins from what seemed impossible odds went unrecognized until years after his retirement. In the fall of 1978, I was blessed to be part of his greatest achievement; that year he led his Lewis County Lions football team to an undefeated regular season. It was truly a season of PRAISE. The preseason papers described our team as a rebuilding year. Written off before the first scrimmage game as too young and too inexperienced to pose a threat to the powerful district foes we would face. Yet the team written off by the experts accomplished a feat not repeated in the ensuing forty-five plus years since it occurred by my home school. Week followed week where we were able to overcome our advisories on the field. Victory followed victory, sometimes the margin was razor thin but each week we managed to be triumphant. At the midpoint of the year, beaten and bruised, barely able to dress the required twenty-two bodies just to hold practice, a miracle occurred. The team we were to play on Friday night called to cancel. An impromptu buy week. Time to heal before finishing the final five games of the season. God provided the miracle we needed just when we needed His intervention. Just as in the days of

Jehoshaphat, He set a winning game plan. Simply rest and He took care of winning. Because of His intervention we completed the regular season without any losses. Now would come the playoffs.

The best sixteen teams in each school classification from across the entire state were to vie for the honor of being named State Champions. Our opponent would be a private military school. As it turned out, they would go on to win the state championship. We were poorly equipped to compete against a team with their talent and resources. Try as we might, we could not overcome this final obstacle of the season.

As the years passed, I have found so many reasons to offer PRAISE to our Lord for the dream season of which He blessed me to be a part. The initial pain of losing followed the recognition and thankfulness of an impossible feat for such a small rural county school as Lewis County High School.

Looking back now I can offer but this small piece of advice. When you face difficulties in this life whether small or large, sing songs of praise to the Lord. Like King Jehoshaphat you will see your enemies defeated. Not only is there victory in praise, but your heart will be lifted, and you will sense peace inside like nothing you have known. God wants to restore the peace you have lost. If you let Him, He will give you a fresh touch of His peace, love, and grace when you praise Him.

PETER GIVES ME HOPE

I want to start with a poem by James Nored called "And God Said If"

If you never felt pain,
    Then how would you know that I'm a Healer?
If you never went through difficulty,
    How would you know that I'm a Deliverer?
If you never had a trial,
    How could you call yourself an overcomer?
If you never felt sadness,

How would you know that I'm a
Comforter?
If you never made a mistake,
How would you know that I'm
forgiving?
If you never were in trouble,
How would you know that I will
come to your rescue?
If you never were broken,
Then how would you know that I can
make you whole?
If you never had a problem,
How would you know that I can
solve them?
If you never had any suffering,

Then how would you know what I
went through?
If you never went through the fire,
Then how would you become pure?
If I gave you all things,
How would you appreciate them?
If I never corrected you,
How would you know that I love
you?
If you had all power,
Then how would you learn to depend
on me?
If your life was perfect,
Then what would you need me for?

(And God Said If; James Nord, 2015:
nextgenerationforchrist.com)

I would like to share with you some of the glorious victories and failures of the disciple who I most relate. You see, like many of you and a certain apostle, I have been blessed with wonderful victories and fantastic flaming failures. My precious wife and our two children are perfect examples of one of my most blessed victories. Truthfully, of my victories this is the one I truly deserved least. I grew up watching those old family shows on TV. I wish I could claim to have been the perfect father, someone like Ward Cleaver on the show, "Leave it to Beaver." Sadly, I would much better resemble poor Darrin Stephens from the TV show, "Bewitched." A lovable screwup trying his best to make it through my days without causing harm or injury. Yet the Lord chose to bless me beyond anything I could ever deserve. This is the victorious Ernie, but like the Apostle Peter I have another side, one I do not care to discuss very often. You see, on the other side of the coin you have work Ernie who loves to go out and play golf with the plant manager and members of his staff. This person fancies himself as accomplished in a sport in which he has never taken a formal lesson. He thinks every shot should soar through the air on a perfect arc and land squarely where aimed. He throws clubs and fusses at himself when his shot travels into the tall grass, woods, or creek bottoms because he attempted to take a short cut.

This Ernie is the author of glorious failures over and over!

Yet, despite my failures, Jesus loves me just as He loved Peter so many years ago.

Journey with me, if you would, as we explore the reasons why "Peter Gives Me Hope!"

Matthew 16 verses 13 - 18 (NIV)

> *When Jesus came to the region of Caesarea Philippi, he asked his disciples, "Who do people say the Son of Man is?" They replied, "Some say John the Baptist; others say Elijah; and still others, Jeremiah or one of the prophets." "But what*

about you?" he asked. "Who do you say I am?" Simon Peter answered, "You are the Messiah, the Son of the living God." Jesus replied, "Blessed are you, Simon son of Jonah, for this was not revealed to you by flesh and blood, but by my Father in heaven. And I tell you that you are Peter, and on this rock I will build my church, and the gates of Hades will not overcome it.

Glorious Victory, right! Can you imagine Jesus saying this to you? Simon, son of Jonah, I am changing your name. From this day forward I will refer to you as "The

Rock", which is what the name Peter (Cephas) meant in the Hebrew language. Not only does He give you a new name but after giving you this glorious name Jesus goes on to say that He plans to build His church on you! Or at least that is what Peter and the other apostles heard.

Next let's turn to Matthew Chapter 14 Verses 25 – 33 (NIV)

> *Shortly before dawn Jesus went out to them, walking on the lake. When the disciples saw him walking on the lake, they were terrified. "It's a ghost," they said, and cried out in fear. But Jesus immediately said to*

them: "Take courage! It is I. Don't be afraid." "Lord, if it's you," Peter replied, "tell me to come to you on the water." "Come," he said. Then Peter got down out of the boat, walked on the water and came toward Jesus But when he saw the wind, he was afraid and, beginning to sink, cried out, "Lord, save me!" Immediately Jesus reached out his hand and caught him. "You of little faith," he said, "why did you doubt?" And when they climbed into the boat, the wind died down. Then those who were in the boat worshiped him, saying, "Truly you are the Son of God."

Wow, this starts out in incredible victory. No person alive had ever walked upon water. Jesus, a prophet for sure, and as the disciples are slowly starting to learn, the Son of God. But Peter at heart is just a simple fisherman. Most likely he grew up poor and on the rough side of town. He has had to work extremely hard for everything. Peter, who likely even spent time in places common to hard working men of the day. Places which now he isn't so proud. Yet it is this very same Peter who calls out to Jesus who is standing outside of the boat on the surface of the water. It is this Peter, the one in which Jesus sees wonderful leadership characteristics. It is this Peter who has the nerve to say, "if it is really You Lord!"

Have you ever said, "if it is really You" to God? I have! Sadly, I have asked this same question several times during my life. When I was young and playing sports and the game was not going the way I wanted it to go, I have asked this question. When I was dating, way more in love with the girl than she with me, I asked this question. When one of my six different employers offered the promotion, I desperately wanted to someone I deemed less qualified, someone who played the game better than myself, sadly I asked this question. I even had the nerve to ask it when Brother Forest asked me to stand in the gap as pastor for the small country church at Ringos Mills. I asked it again when the Lord came to me in a dream and asked if I would give His words back to Him. No, Peter wasn't the only person who ever wanted a little reassurance that he was traveling down the right path with God. But he is the only person to my knowledge to step out of a perfectly good boat and try to walk on water. And he successfully walked on water! Well, for a few steps he stood on top of the water and the waves, his focus fully upon Jesus. Until the worries of this old world got him distracted. Then down he went, defeat snatched from the jaws of victory. Just one more reason for me to see a little bit of Peter when I look in the mirror. I could tell several stories about my life where I accomplished the same feat but let's move forward.

Matthew Chapter 17 verses 1 – 5 (NIV)

> *After six days Jesus took with him Peter, James and John the brother of James, and led them up a high mountain by themselves. There he was transfigured before them. His face shone like the sun, and his clothes became as white as the light. Just then there appeared before them Moses and Elijah, talking with*

> *Jesus. Peter said to Jesus, "Lord, it is good for us to be here. If you wish, I will put up three shelters—one for you, one for Moses and one for Elijah." While he (PETER) was still speaking, a bright cloud covered them, and a voice from the cloud said, "This is my Son, whom I love; with him I am well pleased. Listen to him!*

Have you ever spoken out of turn or answered a question no one was asking? Guilty! Just like poor Peter who answered a question never asked, my tongue has caused me endless embarrassment. This isn't a recent occurrence either. You see I grew up the son of a coach, and not just one of the assistants who help coordinate the many moving parts behind the scenes. No, my father was the head football coach thus, as the eldest son of the head coach I assumed I was also in charge of instructing the young men under my father's guidance. Or at least I did in my younger years. Let me share one such occurrence, it followed a heartbreaking loss by my father's Wurtland Warriors JV basketball team. A very proud 6-year-old version of yours truly waltzed into the locker room and right up to the star of the team (Future Boyd County Head Basketball Coach) and pronounced judgement, *"big-en' if you would have made those free throws we would have won that game!"* Without even knowing how offensive my statement had been, I turned and walked back out of the locker room leaving my precious dad to clean up the mess. Coach Zornes went on to win many games and district championships at the helm of the Boyd County Lions. One thing I can guarantee is, he never allowed his son in the locker room after a hard loss thanks to yours truly. I told you; my mouth works just like Peter's, or at least the way Peter's did during his years as Jesus' disciple.

Looking for another example? Turn to Mark 14:27 - 31 (NIV)

"You will all fall away," Jesus told them, "for it is written:

'I will strike the shepherd, and the sheep will be scattered.'

But after I have risen, I will go ahead of you into Galilee." Peter declared, "Even if all fall away, I will not." "Truly I tell you," Jesus answered, "today—yes, tonight—before the rooster crows twice you yourself will disown me three times." But Peter insisted emphatically, "Even if I have to die with you, I will never disown you." And all the others said the same.

"And all of the others said the same." Have you ever gone along with the group knowing full well the words coming out of your mouth were not your true sentiment? Here Peter makes a grand gesture, and the other ten disciples are quick to add their voices to the chorus. Yes, I did say the other ten. By this time Judas has betrayed Jesus and is leading a mob made up of temple guards, as well as others sent by the chief priests to arrest Jesus. On this night Peter would have been one of eleven instead of twelve. If you have never gone along with the group, you have done much better than yours truly.

In the book of Mark 14: 32 - 41 (NIV) we read about the Garden of Gethsemane experience shared by the disciples. Here it says.

> *They went to a place called Gethsemane, and Jesus said to his disciples, "Sit here while I pray." He took Peter, James and John along with him, and he began to be deeply distressed and troubled. "My soul is overwhelmed with sorrow to the point of death," he said to them. "Stay here and keep watch."*
>
> *Going a little farther, he fell to the ground and prayed that if possible*

the hour might pass from him. "Abba, Father," he said, "everything is possible for you. Take this cup from me. Yet not what I will, but what you will."

Then he returned to his disciples and found them sleeping. "Simon," he said to Peter, "are you asleep? Couldn't you keep watch for one hour? Watch and pray so that you will not fall into temptation. The spirit is willing, but the flesh is weak."

Once more he went away and prayed the same thing. When he came back, he again found them sleeping, because their eyes were heavy. They did not know what to say to him.

Returning the third time, he said to them, "Are you still sleeping and resting? Enough! The hour has come. Look, the Son of Man is delivered into the hands of sinners. Rise! Let us go! Here comes my betrayer!"

On several occasions I have looked lovingly at one of my children as they slept through the pastor's message. Sadly, my eye lids too have grown heavy as the preacher's message seemed endless. This was one of the things I most loved about Brother Forest Tackett. He preached God's Word, and he got right to the point about it too! For Brother Forest a thirty-five-minute message was rare. Yet, when moved by the Lord and fed by the spirit, he spent the time to drive home what God had given him to speak. I did my best to pattern my preaching style after this beautiful man of God who taught me so much during his service at Ringos Mills. Thus, I will take a hint from the passage above where Jesus says to his disciples, the service is ended now for the judgement. This is obviously not a direct quote, but when it is time to go, someone will usually let you know. Before I end this chapter, let us talk about promises not kept. Let me ask a question. I would like to ask if you have kept every promise you ever made. No really, have you ever broken a promise? Hum, my guess is I am squarely in the majority. Peter had a problem keeping his promises too! You see, Peter promised Jesus, he would never forsake Him or disown him. Never is a long time, and obviously a promise to never do something very difficult to keep. Join me in the book of Mark 14:66 - 72 (NIV) where Peter breaks his promise.

> *While Peter was below in the courtyard, one of the servant girls of the high priest came by. When she saw Peter warming himself, she looked closely at him.*

"You also were with that Nazarene, Jesus," she said. But he denied it. "I don't know or understand what you're talking about," he said, and went out into the entryway. When the servant girl saw him there, she said again to those standing around, "This fellow is one of them." Again he denied it.

After a little while, those standing near said to Peter, "Surely you are one of them, for you are a Galilean." He began to call down curses, and he swore to them, "I don't know this man you're talking about." Immediately the rooster crowed the second time. Then Peter remembered the word Jesus had spoken to him: "Before the rooster crows twice you will disown me three times." And he broke down and wept.

- Failure doesn't mean you have blown everything. It simply means you have a hard lesson to learn.
- Failure does not mean you are a permanent loser. It means you are not as smart as you thought you were.
- Failure does not mean you should give up. It means you need the Lord to show you the next step.

- Failure does not mean that God has abandoned you. It means that God has a better plan.

Right now, if I could just take a picture of you and let you see the disbelief on your face. Yet, just look at what God had in store for Peter (and everyone else who made a promise that night which would not be kept). Mark 16: 5-7 (NIV)

> *As they entered the tomb, they saw a young man dressed in a white robe sitting on the right side, and they were alarmed. "Don't be alarmed," he said. "You are looking for Jesus the Nazarene, who was crucified. He*

has risen! He is not here. See the place where they laid him. But go, tell his disciples and Peter, 'He is going ahead of you into Galilee. There you will see him, just as he told you.'"

Despite Peter's many failures, Jesus loved him enough to tell the Angel to specifically mention him by name. I have been blessed to have, like Peter, enjoyed many different failures during my lifetime. Yet He loves me and someday will call me by name. Let me assure you of this one thing. If you call Him Master, if He is your Shepherd, your King of Kings and Lord of Lords, if you have fully given your life to Him, He will call you by name someday also! How glorious will the day be when you see your loved ones awaiting you at Heaven's Gates.

MORE LIKE PETER - (Get Out of the Boat)

Matthew 14:22-31 (NIV) - Jesus Walks on the Water

Immediately Jesus made the disciples get into the boat and go on ahead of him to the other side, while he dismissed the crowd. After he had dismissed them, he went up on a mountainside by himself to pray. Later that night, he was there alone, and the boat was already a considerable distance from land, buffeted by the waves because the wind was against it. Shortly before dawn Jesus went out to them, walking on the lake. When the disciples saw him walking on the lake, they were terrified. "It's a ghost," they said, and cried out in fear. But Jesus immediately said to them: "Take courage! It is I. Don't be afraid."

"Lord, if it's you," Peter replied, "tell me to come to you on the water." "Come," he said.

Then Peter got down out of the boat, walked on the water and came toward Jesus. But when he saw the wind, he was afraid and, beginning to sink, cried out, "Lord, save me!"

Immediately Jesus reached out his hand and caught him. "You of little faith," he said, "why did you doubt?"

In the previous chapter I wrote about victory and failure. Specifically of those of the Apostle Peter and your humble author. I wish to continue the discussion, but I want to point out something maybe you never considered. It takes courage to fail. Thomas Edison was credited with saying something to the likes, "it isn't that I have failed 99 times prior to succeeding with the first light bulb. Rather, I simply found 99 ways not to make a successful light bulb before discovering the correct way." This may not be an exact quote but for my purposes it serves its purpose. Have you ever had the courage to fail. Sadly, failure is an old friend of mine. When I was young, we lived in a trailer behind the Garrison Consolidated School in Lewis County. This school was built during the depression and as its name stated, it had consolidated multiple- room schoolhouses into a single location. After World War II our nation would see a boom in population and this was true of Garrison, Kentucky as well. Thus, the school would see significant additions incorporated into its floor plan by 1960. One of these additions was a cafeteria large enough to hold 300 or so students. Another feature to this new structure was a wonderful, covered porch. It would be on this porch I would teach myself how to kick a football. Unlike other kids of the time who kicked a football in the traditional straight on approach, I was taken with a new "soccer" style approach.

In the 60's and 70's, cheerleaders would throw miniature footballs into the crowd each time the home team scored a touchdown. Being the head coach's son, I was blessed to always seem targeted for one of these little balls.

To kick one of these small balls meant you had to get it to balance on one of the ends while you took your position. Have you ever tried to stand an egg on one of its ends? You can picture the problem I faced. I tried propping it up against rocks but this hurts when you kick the ball. I tried trimming down paper cups and poking holes in the bottom of them so the ball would stand up. Sadly, paper cups don't hold up well to repeated abuse. Finally, I learned to spin them like a top. This worked marvelously. Over and over, I would spin the ball, take my position and attempt to kick the small ball so that it would hit the roof of that porch. Over and over again I failed. Yet eventually I learned the technique necessary to be successful. By the time I had reached the eighth grade, the elementary school football coach had taken notice of my "ability" to kick a ball in a similar fashion to the guys on TV. I would love to say my efforts to self-teach this skill led to a wonderful career kicking a football. In reality I would have some success but not at first. You see, in the last game of the season the coach decided we should give my skill a try. We lined up to kick an extra point. I signaled I was ready. The ball was snapped; it slowly looped its way back to the holder who nearly had to jump to catch it. He placed it on the tee and turned the laces toward the goal. Not until the ball was on the tee did I start my approach, it was eighth grade football, so I had plenty of time. Left, right, plant, kick! The ball hit the center right in the butt and bounced straight up in the air. It was a glorious failure. I took a lot of verbal teasing about my failure. Probably a little like the apostle we will be taking about today.

First: It takes Courage to step out of the boat!

But hop right out onto the surface of the water as Peter did and start walking on water too. Remember, just a few moments earlier the whole group were convinced that Jesus was a ghost. The bible says they were literally crying out with fear when they saw Jesus. What an "about face", from tears of fear, to hey can I join you out there? Yes, I want to be more like Peter, a man of action. By the way, of the twelve apostles only

Peter can say, "hey guys, remember that time that I walked on water in the middle of the Sea of Galilee?" Why is this important you may be asking, after all he did start to sink, and it is true Jesus did scold him for his lack of faith. Yet it was Peter alone who had the courage to step out of the boat.

Jesus in the book of Matthew 16:18 (NIV) says: *"And I tell you that you are Peter, and on this rock I will build my church, and the gates of Hell will not overcome it."* Do you think Jesus would have made this statement if He was worried that Peter would make a mistake? No, Peter was a leader, and leaders stumble and leaders make mistakes. Peter was far from perfect, yet there he stood in the middle of the Sea of Galilee holding Jesus' hand standing on the water. You can do anything through Jesus, just reach out and take his hand and step out of the boat.

Second: It takes confidence to step out of the boat!

Too often I have focused on Peter's confidence, or lack thereof, but step back for just a second. Do you see anyone else jumping out of a perfectly good boat to walk on the water toward Jesus? Can you imagine the other apostles as Peter asks the question, "Lord, if it is you, tell me to come to you on the water." Can't you just see John elbowing Andrew and whispering something like, yeah Peter you just walk on over there to Jesus, it's just the Sea of Galilee and o'yeah it's storming. Peter did not care what the other apostles thought, he saw Jesus and out of the boat he went. How often have you seen something you really wanted to do but wouldn't step out of the boat because you were worried about what other people thought?

My little Angie worries about what others think. Her fear of being judged by others has caused her to miss several opportunities in her life. I went to do something stupid once (we will just leave that alone) and she stopped me and asked " don't you care what people will think?" They say that opposites attract, in our case this is absolutely true. You see, I don't care if it snows oats when it comes to the opinions of others and she constantly worries about the judgement of people who she does not even know. My point is, step out of the boat like Peter, the only person who matters is Jesus!

Finally: It takes faith to step out of the boat!

We get comfortable in our lives, and we resist change to the point of paralysis. If you need a miracle in your life, sometimes you need to step out of the boat trusting Jesus is there to catch you. Miracles don't happen in the boat - You must step out of the boat in faith and trust in Jesus. After all, Jesus is in the Miracle business, large or small!

David could have never killed the giant Goliath if he had worried about what the soldiers around him were thinking. 1 Samuel 17:40 says: Then he took his staff in his hand, chose five smooth stones from the stream, put them in the pouch of his shepherd's bag and, with his sling in his hand, approached the Philistine. (It takes courage)

Joshua could have never conquered Jericho if he had worried about what the children of Israel thought about the plan. Joshua 6:15-16 says: On the seventh day, they got up at daybreak and marched around the city seven times in the same manner, except that on that day they circled the city seven times. The seventh time around, when the priests sounded the trumpet blast, Joshua commanded the army, "Shout! For the Lord has given you the city! (It takes confidence)

Peter would have never dreamed of stepping out of a perfectly good fishing boat until he met Jesus. Jesus changes everything! Is the confidence of Jesus in your heart? Step out of the bondage holding you back from fulfilling your destiny. Jesus has big plans for every one of us, but we must be willing to step out of the boat. (It takes faith)

My father could have never become a head coach if he had played it safe and continued working at Sylvania Electric in Winchester, Kentucky in the maintenance department. Yet it was my mother who urged him to step out of his boat and chase his dreams. Step out he did! Today when you search teams and coaches who have posted undefeated football seasons, you will see his name and his team, the 1978 Lewis County Lions. So, while you may not see my mother's name in print, my dad would tell you it would have never been possible if not for her faith in him and Jesus Christ. What dream is out there waiting for you to step out of your boat of comfort? (Step out of the boat)

Jesus, we pray that you give to us the courage, confidence, and faith as we face the times ahead. Lord, thank you for being willing to face the cross so we can have the hope of salvation. In Jesus name we pray. Amen

LET THE SHEPHERDS TESTIFY, GLORIFY, AND PRAISE GOD

Let me take you back to the year 2010. It was the Sunday before the traditional Nativity Message given by pastors the world over. The Sunday before I was to preach my very first message at Ringos Mills Christian Church. As I sat through Brother Forest's message, I had no thought of the question I would be asked at the end. It was a wonderful and uplifting message about Jesus' love and the glorious gift of the season to which we were currently celebrating. Oddly at the end, after the invitation song and closing prayer, instead of standing by the door to wish everyone a wonderful week, Brother Forest would make his way to the pew where his beautiful wife Ilene awaited. He sit gingerly down by her side. The message had been exhausting for him; it was written on his face. (Of course, I was too wrapped up in the affairs of my life to notice. After all, it is all about me! At this point I had been song leader for several years, pressed into duty when our talented song leader had left to join a larger church. The move had wonderful results for her family as several who had yet to accept Jesus as their Lord and Savior had given their lives to Him in the new church. For me it was an opportunity to serve. While I may not have the musical abilities of my brother Woody, I am loud. Sometimes being loud is enough in a small country church with thirty or so members. Anyway, as I left the stage and approached my seat, Sister Ilene motioned me over. It was a question I will never forget. "Will you give the message next Sunday?" asked Brother Forest. My excuses for not wanting to preach quickly followed his question yet he was undeterred. "Just pray on it and let me know." The discussion was over; the assignment was made by the teacher. The journey for me was just beginning. As directed, I prayed.

The plan for the next Sunday service would begin as thus:

Luke 2:1-20 (NIV) - *And it came to pass in those days that a decree went out from Caesar Augustus that all the world should be registered. This census first took place while Quirinius was governing Syria. So all went to be registered, everyone to his own city.*

Joseph also went up from Galilee, out of the city of Nazareth, into Judea, to the city of David, which is called Bethlehem, because he was of the house and lineage of David, to be registered with Mary, his betrothed wife, who was with child. So it was, that while they were there, the days were completed for her to be delivered. And she brought forth her firstborn Son, and wrapped Him in swaddling clothes, and laid Him in a manger, because there was no room for them in the inn.

Now there were in the same country shepherds living out in the fields, keeping watch over their flock by night. And behold, an angel of the Lord stood before them, and the glory of the Lord shone around them, and they were greatly afraid. Then the angel said to them, "Do not be afraid, for behold, I bring you good tidings of great joy which will be to all people. For there is born to you this day in the city of David a Savior, who is Christ the Lord. And this will be the sign to you: You will find a Babe wrapped in swaddling clothes, lying in a manger." And suddenly there was with the angel a multitude of the heavenly host praising God and saying: "Glory to God in the highest, And on earth peace, goodwill toward men!"

So it was, when the angels had gone away from them into heaven, that the shepherds said to one another, "Let us now go to Bethlehem and see this thing that has come to pass, which the Lord has made known to us." And they came with haste and found Mary and Joseph, and the Babe lying in a manger. Now when they had seen Him, they made widely known the saying which was told them concerning this Child. And all those who heard it marveled at those things which were told them by the shepherds. But Mary kept all these things and pondered them in her heart.

This was all I had planned. Sister Ilene had said it would be fine if I just read the Christmas Story from the book of Luke. It sounded like a great plan to me; I didn't want to preach anyway. But He had a different plan! As I sat down to write out my message He started to pour into me the rest of the message. He told me the birth of the Savior was very important. So much so it divided time as we know it, splitting the calendar into BC and AD. But this same Jesus, born in a manger, sends to us today the same message delivered by the angels to those shepherds of long ago. A message he delivered in person to the Apostle John while exiled to the Isle of Patmos, from the book of Revelation.

> "*Look, I am coming soon! My reward is with me, and I will give to each person according to what they have done. I am the Alpha and the Omega,*

the First and the Last, the Beginning and the End. "Blessed are those who wash their robes, that they may have the right to the tree of life and may go through the gates into the city. Outside are the dogs, those who practice magic arts, the sexually immoral, the murderers, the idolaters and everyone who loves and practices falsehood.

"I, Jesus, have sent my angel to give you this testimony for the churches. I am the Root and the Offspring of David, and the bright Morning Star." The Spirit and the bride say, "Come!" And let the one who hears

say, "Come!" Let the one who is thirsty come; and let the one who wishes take the free gift of the water of life. (Revelation 22:12-17 NIV)

His revelation to me, to those of us who are called to receive the message of the Lord on this day, we have been given a very special job to do. This job, like the job given to simple shepherds who tended their flocks in the field so many years ago on a very special Christmas morning. A truly simple job, but one that is extremely important at the same time. Tell the world about Jesus!

This is the job, this is the day, this is the time. It is both a popular and unpopular job. But we have each been called like those shepherds to testify to the Love it took for God in heaven to send his one and only Son to this earth as a savior for humankind.

It is a job that will require uncomfortable conversations. Conversations with brothers and sisters who do not know Jesus. Conversations we should have had years ago. Conversations with children who may or may not have been raised in church. Children who today do not have time for Jesus because of the pressures brought on by the world we live. To insist grandchildren be raised in church so they can come know the

Love of Jesus. It is the most important job we will ever have… This was the revelation I received for the first Sunday I was called to preach. But He was not finished. He provided guidance for each of us to follow, six simple ways we each can make Christmas about Jesus.

1. Enjoy this wonderful time of the year, do not lose the season in the rush put on by the world.
2. Pause to sense the darkness outside at night and then thank God for sending the light.
3. Start traditions that point to Christ and repeat them religiously each year.

4. Read the Scriptures to your family regularly (especially the words in written in RED).
5. Like Christ, give to those who cannot repay you.
6. Finally, give a gift to Jesus. The gift He so desires, the gift that cost nothing but will result in your eternal salvation. Give Yourself to Jesus!

If you have never accepted Jesus as your Savior what better gift could ever exist, then to give your eternal soul to him. What better time could ever exist than when his children are all gathered to praise and give thanks for His glorious birth.

John 3:16 says, For God so loved the world that he gave his one and only Son, that whoever believes in him shall not perish but have eternal life. Matthew 11:28 says, "Come to me, all you who are weary and burdened, and I will give you rest".

We each carry the burden of our sinfulness through this world. The weight of that sin grows as each day passes. We can never be good enough or work hard enough to earn our way into heaven. It is only when our backs break, and stiff necks bend, and our knees hit the ground that we can receive what God has given to us freely. His Love through Jesus Christ, his One and only Son.

Only through Jesus is forgiveness given for our sins; through burial in baptism with Him, and in a watery grave that covers ALL our past transgressions. Complete Forgiveness through Complete Love - This is what it takes to save you and me. This was the first Christmas gift, given to us freely in a manger in Bethlehem, Jesus A Savior.

This was the first message given to a lay pastor of a small country church. Over the next decade, plus many more messages, would be given to an unworthy servant by his Loving Father. Yet, it was this precious message given first as a reminder of what is most important. A reminder of the first person we will see as we approach Heaven's Gates.

LOVED AND FORGIVEN

Matthew 7:11 says: *If you then, being evil, know how to give good gifts to your children, how much more will your Father who is in heaven give good things to those who ask Him!*

I was blessed to have a loving mother. This statement could be verified by every person who knew my family regardless of the stage of my life. No matter who she was around, her children and their recent victories were her "go to" as a conversation starter. I was blessed to have a loving father also but his pride was more reserved. I never had any doubt as to his love but I doubt he opened many conversations with the current activities of his boys. They have both gone to be with the Lord and it is my true hope to see both of them awaiting me someday when my earthly clock runs out.

How much better gift could anyone receive than Love? Today, if I asked you to choose between wealth and love, which would you choose? If you choose wealth, then those around you will only pretend to care when you are in the room. No one will ever love you, ever! If you choose love, you will have to work hard to earn your way in this life but until your memory fades from eternity everyone who is around you, everyone who speaks your name will do so with Love for you.

Choose love.

During my working years the Lord blessed me with professional mentors. Of these wonderful and talented people who came into my life, several arrived on the scene just when I needed them most. Most of these mentors came across to me as potentially being Christians, yet very few ever spoke of their faith. One of my favorite bosses loved to play golf and was open about having grown up in church. Despite his outstanding athleticism, the "religion" practiced by his parents forbid organized sports. He often spoke with regret and the near hostility he felt toward the God and the church of his youth. Upon graduation he took a job in a stamping mill. Little did he realize despite his hostility toward God, there was a plan set aside for him by a God who deeply loved him. You see, the mill offered educational reimbursement, and my boss was very smart. He was also handsome and quickly caught the attention of a young lady at the plant. She had a different religious background, one which was less hostile to furthering one's education. They would be married; he would further his education, culminating in business with an MBA. Outside of work and with his new wife as cheerleader in tow, he joined every team possible. Success seemed to greet him at his every turn yet, something was missing. For years he searched but despite his best efforts and mountains of trophies as evidence of success he was still hollow, still searching. Sadly, this is but one example of worldly success without God. In the book of Jeremiah, God himself tells Jeremiah He has a plan for each of his children. Plans of good, meaningful success which furthers both the child of God as well as God's kingdom plans. My friend and his new wife attend church together. Evidence that it is never too late to find your way into God's plans.

This is the choice God is asking us to make. Love Me as I have Loved You! How has God loved me you may ask? He gave His very Son as a sacrifice so you might spend eternity in heaven with Him. Plus, He gave each of us the gift of choice so we might find forgiveness.

Blessed beyond human understanding

At this point in my life, I have had the opportunity to witness and even partake in the human version of inheritance. I watched as some received nothing but debt from their loved ones who have passed while others received various levels of wealth. Blessed is the person who does not inherit debt when loved ones pass from this life to the next.

An inheritance of debt:

My feeble way of explaining hell would be to compare it to an inheritance of utter debt. Debt so incredibly large one can never escape its grasp. Unforgivable debt where bankruptcy is impossible. Imagine that you have worked all of your life to provide for your family and just when it looks like you have provided a nest egg of support for yourself, you find out that everything that you have, everything you have worked for, all of your possessions are suddenly forfeited because of the debt incurred by another. To make it worse, what you have is not enough and you have to continue to work until the end of your days. Yet even then all your effort will not be enough. You find out not only will you have to forfeit everything, but your children will also inherit this punishment. This is a form of Hell on earth and just the thought of it scares me to death.

An inheritance of reward:

Heaven on the other hand is the blessed inheritance that we dream about, a rich relative that you only barely remember passes and leaves you everything. Only in Heaven not only do you receive a mansion, and golden streets, and gates of pearl but more importantly, you get to spend it with Jesus and the Father, and all those you love. A blessing of never again knowing want; never again knowing need. Eternally Blessed!

Forgiveness without limit

My mother was precious to me. I know she was aware of my feelings. Yet since her passing, I have come to recognize multiple times when my actions must have hurt her deeply. I did not hurt her to be cruel; love does not act in such a manner. I like to hope my poor choices which led to her disappointment were all part of the process of becoming an adult. But during my recent reflection, even in adulthood I made decisions which caused her pain. This is sometimes the way life goes. I had the misfortune to set on the jury of a capital murder trial. A wife had murdered her husband and tried to hide his body to escape suspicion. She was quite ingenious concerning the level of subterfuge she was able to put together between the time she fired the fatal bullet and her flight from justice but that is another story. As I sat in the jury box listening to the evidence presented it seemed odd to me the sheer volume of anecdotal evidence focused on the murdered man's love for his momma. The prosecuting attorney told us how he would call his momma every night before she went to bed. How at the age of 50+ he was still a regular at both her breakfast and supper table. How he would regularly show up with new trinkets for her house. When a faucet would start to leak, he was "Johnny on the spot" installing a new faucet for his dear sweet momma.

The defense attorney would focus on his more nefarious side. They wanted to place a focus on the fact that momma might not have any leaky faucets, but every fixture in his house leaked despite regular rounds of pleading by his wife. They also wanted to point out that when he was not at work or with momma, he had a special someone who lived in a charming home, drove a nice automobile, and dressed extraordinarily nice, despite not holding down a job. They also pointed to the gun cabinets in the house which were used not to hold guns but earnings everyone's favorite uncle was not supposed to know about.

It was a marriage born when they were young. They both worked hard to become what the world would describe as successful. It was a home where God was unknown and uninvited. Even on holidays when other families attend church, they never darken the doors. The world measures success in a way completely opposite to the way God measures success. Their success cost him his life and her freedom. Despite everything which came out during the trial, the affair, the stolen goods, the neglect, and abuse, the last thing his momma would say before she left the stand as the trial neared its end was, "I will love him until the day I die."

Unconditional Love is not something reserved for mothers and fathers. It took unconditional love to send you and me a savior named Jesus Christ. This was God's unconditional love born for the sole purpose of taking every sin we have ever committed, and every sin we will ever commit upon himself, so we might be worthy of standing at those Heavenly Gates someday.

ARE YOU IN HIM?

As I progress through the pages of this book, I must renew my focus on the purpose to which it is written. In Paul's letter to the Ephesians, he alludes to the gift we receive through our acceptance of Him. Part of the gift which awaits those who believe without any doubt in their heart is the reunion of our hearts to those whom we held so dear. What a glorious reunion that will be when our journey through life leads us to those gates made of pearl. There to be joined with those whom we love, those who have gone on before, those who wait at the gates for our arrival.

Ephesians Chapter 1 Verses 1-14 (NKJV)

Paul, an apostle of Jesus Christ by the will of God,

To the saints who are in Ephesus, and faithful in Christ Jesus:

Grace to you and peace from God our Father and the Lord Jesus Christ.

Blessed be the God and Father of our Lord Jesus Christ, who has blessed us with every spiritual blessing in the heavenly places in Christ, just as He chose us in Him before the foundation of the world, that we should be holy and without blame before Him in love, having predestined us to adoption as sons by Jesus Christ to Himself, according to the good pleasure of His will, to the praise of the glory of His grace, by which He made us accepted in the Beloved. In Him we have redemption through His blood, the forgiveness of sins, according to the riches of His grace which He made to abound toward us in all wisdom and prudence, having made known to us the mystery of His will, according to His good pleasure which He purposed in Himself, that in the dispensation of the fullness of the times He might gather together in one all things in Christ, both which are in heaven and which are on earth—in Him. In Him also we have obtained an inheritance, being predestined according to the purpose of Him who works all things according to the counsel of His will, that we who first trusted in Christ should be to the praise of His glory.

In Him you also trusted, after you heard the word of truth, the gospel of your salvation; in whom also, having believed, you were sealed with the Holy Spirit of promise, who is the guarantee of our inheritance until the redemption of the purchased possession, to the praise of His glory.

Chosen First

I used to love recess and gym; they were my favorite parts of school. From my earliest memory of school, my focus was on the school yard not on the classroom. I grew up in a family of athletes and when I went to school, that served me very well at recess time. Despite having parents who were teachers, I viewed the classroom and schoolwork as the necessary stipulation which made sports accessible. At recess we would play softball, football, dodgeball, or basketball. Choosing sides was a positive experience for me as for the most part ,I was either doing the choosing or the one picked very early.

I would love to write on these pages whether I was chosen first or last, it never mattered when I was growing up. This would be an incredible lie. Like every other child standing there waiting to be chosen, I wanted to be picked first. Plus, being picked first meant you weren't just on the team, getting to play your preferred position. No, being picked first meant you had a say in who else would be picked for the team. You didn't just get to be part of the supporting cast; you were responsible for the victory.

This is exactly the way it was with God. He carefully laid out his plans of creation, and he understood everything about his creation. He designed you and me for the place where he lives and then he laid the foundations of the universe in which we live. He provided everything we needed to create the garden paradise we know today. He was the ultimate team captain, choosing a team which would win the most important game of all time. The game of eternal life where the stakes are truly heaven or hell. Yes, He knew we would falter. He understood we would sin. He knew before he breathed life into Adam we would need a redeemer. He laid out the path of salvation before he placed the first star in the heavens. Why, because he intended heaven for you and me. But unlike those school yard teams where two of the most popular kids choose the fate of the mass of kids hoping to be picked. On

God's team you get to choose! At Heaven's Gates, loved ones long past and a Father like no earthly father who has ever lived, await your choice; Heaven or Hell chosen of our own freewill as our eternal destination.

Final Choice

In the book by Luke, written in Red Letters, we read:

> *"In the same way, I tell you, there is rejoicing in the presence of the angels of God over one sinner who repents." (Luke 15:10 NIV)*

Can we agree on the fact, despite our best efforts none of us is perfect. I truly hope we can agree on this point. You see it is so important we agree on the fact that none of us is perfect. Not me for sure, but not you either. In fact, no person we have ever known no matter how good we thought they were, qualified as "perfect." Because of this simple fact, none of us could ever go to heaven because the requirement to go to Heaven is perfection. But Heaven would be a lonely place if only perfect people were allowed to go there. This is why we have Jesus. He chose to give his life as an atonement for all of us, and all our sins. He is the reason we can choose to be on God's team. He is the "root cause" there are celebrations in Heaven when each sinner repents. You see, God chose YOU to be on His team first. He did this by sending His

Son to die for your sins. How great it is when you think about it, just like in that schoolyard so many years ago. God has picked you first and now it is your job to help pick the rest of the team. Who have you chosen? Who have you told about Jesus? Who have you told about the wonderful gift of forgiveness of sin? Is your whole family on the team? If not, can I ask why? As Jesus hung from the cross, He chose to forgive a thief who by the way, as history tells us, was also guilty of manslaughter as someone died during the robbery. No one really talks about it much, but Barabbas, the man who Pilot released instead of Jesus was a murderer. When did he commit his murder? He was the one who killed the man being robbed.

The two thieves who were hanging on Jesus' right and left were but his accomplices. Yet Jesus forgave him and promised him a place in paradise. Now if Jesus can forgive him, surely he can forgive that family member nobody talks about, and He can forgive you too for having not already witnessed to them.

Heaven's Gates, who will be there waiting for you? I would personally like to have my whole family standing there waiting for me.

INVITATION:

We have reached the time in the book when it is time to choose teams. However, this time the team captains do not get to choose the players but rather, the players get to choose the captain. Whose team will you choose to join? There is a rule to His wonderful master plan. You see, you must choose! It is the one rule God made, and no one can escape! You must consciously choose whether to accept Jesus as your team captain or choose to reject Him. ***You - have - to - choose!***

Standing before you are the gates of pearl. Just inside await those whom you have loved during this lifetime. Beloved mothers and fathers waiting with great anticipation of your choice. Grandmothers and grandfathers who held your fingers as you took those early unsure steps now wait and hope to see you again. But again, there is God's rule, you must choose to accept Jesus as your Lord and Savior. It is not my rule and there is no getting around it.

Whoever believes and is baptized will be saved, but whoever does not believe will be condemned. Mark 16:16 (NIV)

ACKNOWLEDGEMENT:

It is my sincere hope you found blessings hidden in the words of this book. Should the Lord choose to share any future words through his servant at the small country church in Ringos Mills, Kentucky and should you choose to read them, I pray you will be equally blessed. As I have quoted before, so let me share again the words of the book of Isaiah which say, “So shall My word be that goes forth from My mouth; It shall not return to Me void (empty, without fruit) But it shall accomplish what I please, And it shall prosper in the thing for which I sent it.” (Isaiah 55:11 NKJV)

I want to thank Angie and Ilene Tackett for proofreading the content of every book before release. I love to testify to the fact these wonderful women of God have forgotten more bible than I will ever know. I also want to thank Marquetta Flaugher again. Marquetta does such a wonderful job editing and making the structure of these books readable. It is with their approval that I send these words off to press.

I also want to express my thanks to my wife Angie who carefully reads the words I put on the page. She checks and double checks both the accuracy of my work and my memory. We are very thankful the Lord has led you to read the words of a lay pastor and his wife from a small country church in the foothills of eastern Kentucky. It is our hope to share these words with any who have yet to choose Jesus as their Lord and Savior through the words and pages of this book and each of its five predecessors.

APPENDIX

A Question in the Crowd: Who Is This? by Marvin A. McMickle President of Colgate Rochester Crozer Divinity School. Preaching.com

And God Said If; James Nord, 2015: nextgenerationforchrist.com

Robinson, Ernie: Trilogy Publishing 2022 Words of Forgiveness in a Small Country Church

New International Version (NIV) Holy Bible, New International Version®, NIV® Copyright ©1973, 1978, 1984, 2011 by

LAST WORD

Let me ask a simple question. Are you in need of His touch today? Do you feel like you have lost your way and there is no road you can take that will bring you back home? God offers complete forgiveness and eternal salvation if you will but step out into that aisle and walk these few steps from you to me. Won't you Claim your birthright today, He is waiting for you. He is waiting at Heaven's Gates!

ABOUT THE WRITER

Over the past five books I have searched for an accurate way to describe the servant of the Lord chosen to put His words to print. I like to think of myself as the oldest son of a gifted football coach and history teacher. A person who grew up in the sports locker rooms of Boyd, Greenup, and Lewis Counties more so than the pews and classrooms of God's houses in rural Eastern Kentucky. As I have mentioned, my very first bed resided in a small apartment above a basketball gymnasium in Winchester, Kentucky. Sports was not just all I knew growing up, it was who I was.

On the other hand, I was also the oldest son of a book worm, first grade teacher and reading specialist who loved Jesus and insisted I attend church with her every time the doors opened. My father, the football coach, made sure I was at my mother's side. Thus, two lives intertwined into one person. One focused on chasing a ball and the other attending church and a pursuit of scholastic excellence. Let me assure you that discussions held inside a sports locker room are significantly different than church classroom discussions, and half-time motivational speeches given by coaches regardless of the sport are significantly dissimilar to Sunday morning emotional pleas from the pulpits of small country churches. Yet there I was, one foot in each world.

As I aged, my lust for sports mellowed within me to admiration. My competitive edge shifted to the world of industry and Quality Assurance. Winning in my world meant the customer received a product which performed superior to their expectations. Along the way I found myself blessed to sit in boardrooms and offices of people who shared my same commitment. It was during this time the Lord pressed me into His service. A small country church whose pastor needed to step aside due to health reasons. A simple Christian whose mother and father had impressed upon him a sense of duty and responsibility. A church which inhabited but a wide spot on a road, a House of the Lord with thirty or so members. A church in which I would raise my family and praise my Heavenly Father.

Who is the writer of the book you have just finished? A simple servant who hopes to find a Loving God waiting for him with arms wide open standing just outside the Gates of Heaven.

This said, I truly hope the Lord blesses you through the words of this book. May God Bless You through the words of His newest work, "Meet Me at Heaven's Gates."

To access other works by the author please search, "Books by Ernie Robinson" at Amazon.com

Book titles by the author include:

- Words of Forgiveness in a Small Country Church
- Words of Grace in a Small Country Church
- Jesus: Getting to know Him in a Small Country Church
- Backroads and Small Country Churches
- You Are Loved in a Small Country Church

Made in the USA
Coppell, TX
11 June 2026

80959805R00121